I0435364

# *Teaching in a rural primary school*

## One year is not enough

## W. Val Chambers

Copyright © 2015, W. Val Chambers

ISBN-13: 978-1506086385
ISBN-10: 1506086381

# Contents

# Introduction

They say that teachers are born, not made. If you are a teacher at heart, when the itch gets to you, you are bound to scratch. The real teacher's obsession is akin to the prophet's. As the ancient prophet, Amos of Tekoa, said, "The lion has roared; who will not fear? The Lord God has spoken; who can but prophesy?"

The irresistible itch to teach caught me in 1976 after I had left teaching for two years. I had come back to Jamaica in 1972 with a doctorate from Vanderbilt University in Biblical Studies, had taught at West Indies College and had worked as an organizer for the government literacy program. I had resigned both positions under pressure, not learning the lesson history has taught ever so clearly: If you speak like a prophet you will suffer like a prophet.

To find a job is often as difficult for the overqualified as it is for the person without the necessary certification. The secondary schools in the western end of the island where I was living would not hire me. At Knockalva Secondary the vice-principal quickly filled the post after I had applied. The head at Cornwall College coldly asked me to make an application. The principal at Green Island Secondary xeroxed my degrees and assured me of a place—and finally advised me that the Ministry of Education said it was too late. When the principal left I applied for the job of principal which had become vacant. I hadn't the ghost of a chance; the ex-principal had recommended his friend for the post.

Cajoled into applying to teach English and Literature at Moneague Teachers' College I reluctantly complied. The principal, a man with a doctorate himself, seemed intimidated by my presence and I ended up interviewing him instead of the other way round. I am still to get a reply to the application I was asked to make.

Not inclined to take a job in the city I hit on a wonderful idea. The Principal at Claremont All Age had expressed dismay that no one would hire me though teams kept going abroad to recruit expatriate teachers. Why not ask him, I thought, to hire me? I had been reading widely on education but was not strictly "qualified" in education. The exposure in teaching in a primary school would be a marvelous piece of qualification and I would learn the problems and prospects firsthand. When I filled out the application, I was inclined to put a first degree as my qualification. Pushed by the principal I put my qualification as M.A., fearful that even the Ministry of Education would think me too qualified. That explains why they were not aware they had someone with a Ph.D. teaching in one of their primary schools.

# CHAPTER 1

## "To Press the Business On"

Only the last mile or so of the road from Lucea to Claremont was really bad. But by now I had become an expert in driving on substandard Jamaican roads. My 1972 Ford Capri was in excellent condition and the roads did not frighten me unduly. As I rounded the deep corner at Old Peak, having savored as in childhood the view overlooking Mosquito Cove harbor and Montego Bay I began to wonder how people would accept me as a seventh-grade teacher in a village in the backwoods of Jamaica.

The long awaited day had come, and after worship exercises and introductions I stood before a class of seventeen pre-teenagers to see if it was true that education was possible in these conditions if the teacher could find a way.

My experiences in teaching was at the high school and college levels. Why should I not be able to teach a twelve-year-old as easily as I could an older high school child? I had several weeks before me to find out.

There was no textbook, no module for me to follow. I was going to find my way, if there was a way; and I was convinced there was a way. First I was going to find out what the students could do and figure out what I could do with them.

I had bought the day's edition of *The Daily Gleaner* and I decided to have them read an article of their choice. Rose read, in a quiet pleasant diction, an article entitled "Love Is the Meaning of Socialism". All the students, except Lascelles, could read; and even he knew some words. I had read in the press that the schools were teeming with non-readers. It certainly was not true of this school.

The situation I found was nearer to what I remember at the primary school I attended a mile and a half away over two decades before. Everyone except those regarded as retarded could read. Those I remember could recite poems brilliantly. They learned to count and figure (even to make change), but they resisted every attempt to make writing and books disturb their lives. The teachers back then ignored them as much as possible while they flogged and abused those they felt had the gift of literacy. How we envied them sometimes. They were eligible for a flogging only when they did some great evil—which to some teachers would be anything from throwing a stone to wielding a fist.

The children, I discovered, found it easier to read than talk with an adult. But this first day they did not seem reluctant to let us get to know each other. I noticed that among the boys Leroy seemed shy, but most of them would do some talking. Delvan, at eleven, was one of the youngest, and the liveliest and most mischievous in the class. I learned from our discussions that he had an older brother, Joseph, who would be joining the class on the second day.

"Where is your father?" I asked Delvan.

"Gone to shut-eye country, sir." I hadn't remembered the expression. It all came back now and I discovered that I was about to start re-learning a language I knew so well as a boy.

"Father dead and mother deaf," one boy said with amusement. They explained to me that Delvan's mother was indeed deaf and was living in Trelawny, forty or fifty miles from their village. Delvan did not regard the boy's alliterative reference to his dead father and his deaf mother with amusement. He was hurt and angry. Anger came easily to Delvan. He was a small boy and physically no match for the other boys in the class; but he was their superior in passion. Luckily for them, he could easily have a good cry. Today would be a day for weeping; tomorrow it could be war.

I was eager to know what did or could make these students tick. What were the things that were of special interest to them? Some of them thought I wanted to know what they wanted to be when they grew up. Rose, Gail and Clayva were interested in teaching, Janet in nursing, Glenville in farming, Carl in electronics, Edval in welding and Winston in mechanics. There were at least two imaginative types in the class. Rose, the teacher, was interested in poetry and Hyacinth was fascinated by the moon. Lascelles who loved driving, wanted to be a pilot. Sheila was interested in education but her older sister, Sandra, was simply interested in money. Delvan's special interest was Jamaican history; Courtney's consuming passion was cricket, and he had ambitions to be one of the greatest. Eight years later I met a younger brother of his who was on the Rusea's High School team which was massacred by island champions St. Elizabeth Technical.

Later in the day I organized a Talent Parade. Lascelles was the star performer. Hesitant in his academic performance in class, Lascelles was a charismatic figure on stage, a story-teller extraordinaire. True to Jamaican tradition Lascelles, called Vin by his classmates, threw away all pretensions of speaking Standard English when he was telling a story. Vin's story, about "de duppy horse" and "de good horse" was in dialect and delighted the class.

During riddle time one boy came up with one I hadn't heard before: "Why does a baby and a plane resemble?" Answer: "The plane flies from city to city and the baby goes from tittty to titty." I was quite taken aback that he could dare give that riddle. Then I noticed that not one student was shocked. I hid my own shock under a smile and let the riddle pass. *Where ignorance is bliss...*, I thought. After all, while abroad I had even been called by a Jamaican badword. At Vanderbilt University I had met a Bahamian who was studying at Fisk University. He never, as far as I know, learned my name. He always greeted me with that famous Jamaican curse word, which became, to my amusement, my name. So why now should I fly into a rage to refine the sensibilities of these eleven and twelve- year-olds? What I do know is that my own primary school teacher would have given that boy an unforgettable lashing.

When I myself was a student at Jericho school most of us were much more aware of what was proper than this bunch. "Teacher," the unforgettable E. W. McHayle, certainly saw to that. During a school concert, Harry, a boy who recently joined our school from somewhere in Westmoreland, the neighboring parish (but then a world away), sang a Westmoreland song one day when Teacher was absent:

> Blessed assurance, Westmoreland is mine
> With plenty of breadfruit and gad-a-mi too...
> What will young girls do when Kingston
> Man gone?

When Teacher returned Miss Gayle put the story of the atrocity into his lap. Teacher, incredulous that the new boy could so despoil his decorous school with such obscene lyrics, gave Harry a beating he is not likely to forget.

There was no logical reason for me to accept the hypocrisies of the forties and fifties as a model for 1976. When my first day ended I knew I was just beginning to learn. I was going to love these children, and together we were going to explore and learn.

Claremont is a little village tucked away into a little corner of Hanover, about two miles from the coast road that leads from Montego Bay to Lucea to the West. By car the village is reached by way of Jericho which is a mile and a half away. The road in from Jericho was in a state of perpetual disrepair. When the rains came, parts of the road simply disappeared.

The village commands a pleasant view of about twelve miles of coastline towards Montego Bay. In the nights the lights string themselves out around the harbor for one of the truly spectacular views on the island. But if Montego Bay, the great tourist city, is only fifteen or so miles away as the crow flies, the social environment of the village is miles and perhaps half a century away.

Claremont is little changed now from when I was a boy. It must have been much the same when my mother attended school here in the 1920s. The roads could hardly have been worse and people still live in the fatalistic universe in which childbearing is an accident of girlhood. According to the village folklore, students here cannot expect to pass scholarship examinations (or any other examination for that matter) because some evil charm has been placed at the gate of the school. It had been years since a student from Claremont got a chance to get a high school education.

The seventh grade shared a small building with grades eight and nine which sat and were taught together. What was once a lab was locked away behind our classroom. The tiny library also adjoined Grade Seven. The books were kept under tight security. But I was beginning to take something out of the students. Sooner or later I was going to face the problem of putting something in. Effective teaching would hardly be possible without books. I vowed to break the rules of the library and let the students in—permanently.

On Tuesday morning I started the class with the latest news, ascertaining that Joseph who was absent on the first day could read. I had bought the newspapers from Lucea, six miles away. Till the sixties *The Daily Gleaner* had a regular outlet in Jericho where people from Claremont took their letters. I seem to remember as a boy a newspaper seller going to Claremont.

My grandfather was a regular subscriber to *The Gleaner* which I began to read from I was nine or so. Now a newspaper in Claremont was something for wrapping salted fish. A newspaper so early in the morning to my students must have been like Santa Claus in July. I ran through the headlines, read some news, including sports in which the boys were deeply interested.

The writing exercise for the morning was a simple one: "What I want to do this term." The new boy, Joseph, could answer that in one sentence, enough to impress any new teacher: "I want to enjoy my lessons very much." Courtney was more ambitious. He wrote: "I want to be well educated this term." Glenville wanted to be "the brightest boy in the class," ignoring heredity, background and all previous history. He also wanted, more modestly, to be a good cricketer and to learn to drive. Hyacinth simply wanted an opportunity to visit the capital. Kingston after all, to a country child, is not far removed from the center of the universe, and it is a status symbol when one finally gets there. Gail would want nothing better than to learn to do mathematics, a subject in which she was quite weak. Janet, Sandra and a number of others would like to pass the Common Entrance in order to go to high school. Clayva added that she would like to be different and read many books. Lintel, a small, quiet boy, put it succinctly: "I want to enjoy myself with cricket and education." Lascelles, whom I had judged a non-reader on the first day, would like to be the best batsman and "the best *runna* in the world."

Spanish class consisted of the few words of greeting, (How are you? Very well thank you. Many thanks. Good morning, students. Good afternoon teacher. Good. Bad) which the children loved. Cracking a new language code was a great delight, especially for Delvan who wanted to go beyond the class and to try to say things the class was not taught as yet.

It was my duty the first week to conduct the elections for the Seventh Grade Club. The only political interest the boys had in the proceedings was to pool their votes against Hyacinth, the attractive, ambitious outsider who was the niece of the principal. She ran for president and lost. She ran for secretary with the same result, all to the delight of the boys. When someone remembered that Joseph was planning to leave for Trelawny the following week, they remem-bered Hyacinth, whose political career was now in shambles, with compassion. They voted her secretary with a large majority.

On Wednesday morning I taught poetry to the joint grade eight and nine class, then did the same in grade seven. I gave them leads, told them they did not have to use rhymes. Some of the first efforts were studies in disaster. Wrote one child in a piece he described as a poem on "The Cow": "The cow is a very common animal. They are hudge animal they have a long tail. All cows have ticks on them garling [the local name for the egret] came and pick them off the cows. The cows are feed on grass and drink water." Sheila's effort did not respect the usual break-up into lines but had a sense of metaphor and showed some exposure to literature. Her poem:

> A gentle breeze came and rock
> the tree it swade and shivered to
> the breeze.
> It feels like a stone, it is very lovely watching
> a tree dancing in the breeze.

Winston who was to prove an infrequent visitor to school handled poetry like an old pro. His poem was decorated with a branch on which stood a little bird. The poem was entitled "The Bird".

> The sounds of the birds are echoing in the treetop,
> It sounds so sweet and nice into my ears,
> But when I feels like eating one, I shew a stone at them.
>
> When I sit in the garden at noon,
> The birds all look like flower bloom.
> They shake and they spin and

they whistle so sweetly,
Up to the passers passing by stop to
take a look.

The birds move as fast as the wind.
And from tree to tree they
sing and dance.
The bird were as happy as can be
Especially when it is guinep time.

Essay time again. I asked the children to write about themselves. Delvan began, to the amusement of himself and others: "I am a bad boy. I like nice girls to press…" He vigorously and quickly rubbed out the rest as I approached him. I suspected he had written, "…the business on me." The idea of "pressing the business on" comes from a ring game we have played in the region since childhood. Each player gets a partner and joins a ring and sings:

I bought a horse and hired a gig
That all the world may have a jig
And I will do what'er I can
To press the business on.
To press the business on
To press the business on
And I will do what'er I can
To press the business on.

At the first repetition of "To press the business on" boy and girl face each other clapping. At the next to the last line they hold each other and spin around, the boy going to the left and the girl going to the right, and to another partner. The game finishes when boy and girl get back to their original partner. A close hold on a girl came to be known as "pressing the business on". Shy and eleven, Delvan was only delighted in pressing the business on in theory.

During reading time I took the children to explore the little school library by our classroom, actually a little room under lock and key most of the time. Some could find nothing interesting to read. Hyacinth, for instance, wasn't in the mood. But a number of them concentrated diligently. Too many chose easy readers. Lascelles, the least competent, took a book with only a few words and soon announced that he had read one book already.

When the period was finished I asked them to write about what they had read or to give an account of what they were doing during the period.

A few settled down to write immediately. Some took a long time to start, and others gave every indication that they were not interested in starting at all. A half an hour before twelve I announced that no one would be going home before writing a page. Most of them beat the clock. All were finished before ten minutes after twelve. Sandra, a diligent reader, turned in over two pages. But I felt a little disappointed that the week was drawing to a close and I had not succeeded in getting them to write with delight.

On Friday afternoon I asked the students to write a summary of the events of the week in the form of a letter to their teacher. They were to say what they personally thought about it. Even Gail, the matriarch of the class was careful to voice great appreciation for her teacher.

Dear Teacher,
      From you have been here with us from Monday I enjoy being with you
and would like to be with you forever.
From since the term have began I like the way in which it is running, but one thing I don't like when they have different teachers for different subjects. I also like the way in which you co-operate with all of us. I appreciated you very much.

Your Student
Gail Gordon.

On impulse I thought I'd respond to Gail's letter

Dear Gail,
      What a week I have had! It is, I think, the beginning of good things. I hope you will develop the qualities of leadership which you so richly possess. Read some more and you will make me happy.

Your Teacher,
W.Val Chambers

The principal had just started to experiment with subject teaching in his primary school. The children were learning to adjust to it. Gail did not like it; and neither did Lintel.

Dear Mr. Chambers,

I apreacheate you very much. I am willing to corporate with you this term. if I would have the chance to be with you all the time I would. I like the weak and the Subject very much. but one thing I don't like the exchanging of teachers. I see you as a nice man and a kind man I would like you to teach us more Spanish I also thanked you for those you teach us already.

Your Student
Lintel.

Joseph claimed to be giving a review of the week and proceeded to give a character analysis of his teacher.

Dear Mr. Chambers,

I would like to tell you about the Week review. First I enjoy myself very much with you you taught us a lot of things and I am glad that you is my teacher. I wish you could be our teacher always. I like when you teaches me you are the best teacher that Ever teaches us. I am very glad that you decide to take over our class. you are a very nice man. you don't rough us as others would do I like the way how you teach us you are very faithful

I am the Same
Joseph Jackson

My response said something about Joseph's character.

Dear Joseph,

I enjoyed having you in class after missing you the first day. I appreciate how you do your work promptly and cooperate in class. Even though you do not smile very much I can see that you have a good heart. You won't know how I will miss you if you have to go to Trelawny.

Your teacher,
W.Val Chambers

Carl, like Joseph, took up the theme of teachers being rough to students. The assessment of the teacher's ability should, however, be taken with the grain of salt it deserves under the circumstances.

Dear Teacher,
I would like to tell how I spend the week with you. I like how you teach us. you are a very good teacher. you are a very nice man, I like the way you talk to us, you do not talk to us rought like some other teacher's. I do not like how some of the Children are talking when you is talking to us. I would like you to teach us all the time I like Spanish you teaches us I do not have any things else.
Your
Student
Carl

Some students did not have much to say except, like Leroy, that they enjoyed the week and liked Spanish and would like to learn more. They all tended to rate learning by how much enjoyment it gave them. Barbara was one example.

Dear Teacher,

From since the week had began. I enjoy myself very much. I learn much about Mathematics and good news from the Gleaner. I enjoy the week not too good I enjoy the spanish very much. Today I read a lot of books I didn't like what you gave us to do at all. Some of the children them are not going on good today.

Barbara Gray

And this from a child who forgot to sign her name:

Dear Teacher,

I enjoy being with you. I enjoy english with you and reading. I dont enjoy myself on friday. I dont enjoy playing. Sometimes I enjoy myself with you and sometimes not. When I am happy I enjoy myself. But when am not happy I dont enjoy myself.

Hyacinth who could not make up her mind whether she should call herself Hyacinth or Sharon noted with pleasure that her teacher did not flog anyone for a whole week.

Dear Sir,

I enjoy the week with my teacher very much with my teacher. I was pleased to see that he didn't beat this week. I enjoy the music that Miss Donaldson gave us.

Your student
Sharon Campbell

Honest Sandra and forthright Delvan refused to tell me only pleasant things.

Dear Teacher,

I am going to tell you about what I like this week and what I dont like. First I like the Spanish teaching, the Reading, the english the mathematics and the social study and everything. What I don't like this week is some of the children were going on too bad especially today. The children were going on the worst than every today also my self I love my teacher very much.

your same
Sandra Haughton

For my Seventh Grade class I chose poetry for the period called "Optional" (when a teacher elects to do whatever he wants to do). Delvan gave the name Optional to his favorite subject.

Dear Teacher,

I don't like some of the things in class but any way I like some. Firstly I don't like when you ask Vin a question and he don't want to answer, but when you ask anybody else Vin is the first one to answer. Mr Puss when you ask him a question he is always whispering. I don't like that although I do that sometimes but not seldom. I enjoy Optional and every subject that you teach us, Optional is my favorite.

that All senor
Your alumnos
Delvan

Courtney and Sheila seemed from their letters to be interested in the learning process. Courtney's writing was not often bothered by disruptive things like punctuation marks. His letter:

Dear Teacher

I spend the week not too happy and not too unhappy I read libruary book quite as many as I could read I read about Sleeping bueaty, Brenda helps grand mother and nue hat and old hat and many other more and and my own book too and out teacher I like him very much

you student
Courtney Brown

Eleven-year-old Sheila had an impish shyness. In between she was a serious student. Years later when I saw her in her Rusea's High School uniform she was still a shy little girl.

> Dear teacher,
> I hope you enjoy yourself being with us the week. I enjoy myself being with you very nice. I like the way you are teaching us interesting things. You teach us about the Gleaner in the mornings that we can know what is happening in the world. I love to do Mathematics and reading. Loving teacher Mr. Chamber.
>
> Your Student
> Sheila Haughton

Soon she would be dropping some of her formality and writing to me like a friend. *"Whats cooking in the golden kitchen of yours I hope it is Dumplin, mutton currygoat and rice and peas. It seems like you love grade 9 children more than us. it seems that you is J.G.L. Jamaica Greatest Lover you love everybody. tell me who you love best in grade 7. I think I love you the best. But I am not behaviouring quite well please forgive me. you must play with us in PE too. Because we are under heavy manners. I am sorry that you is not teaching us today. Preach on Pastor Dear sir."*

Clayva was a pleasant girl, but she did not like to play. She was, however, popular enough to be voted president of the Class Club. She confided in her letter that I had told her "lots of different thing about Jamaica and other countries." She extended an invitation to visit her home—I suspect because she knew she is a distant relative, her grandmother being a cousin of my mother's.

Janet, a trying student, was very emphatic she did not want me to visit her home. But it was not a sign of hospitality for she brought me some lovely mangoes during the week.

Dear Teacher,

I enjoyed your teaching since you have been here. I don't like how you are leaving our class and go to another class.

You teaches us how to read news paper. I don't like how so many teachers are teaching somany subjects. I like how you are kind to us and dont punish us you are so loving and sweet I dont want you to leave us.

Your same
Janet Brown

At the close of the week even the weakest reader in the Class, Lascelles, was reading and liking it. He told me in his faltering letter, "When you are teaching me I feel nice."

# CHAPTER 2

## "The Past Is Deep"

Despite Sheila's confidence that I loved Grade Nine more than her class I regarded Grade Seven as my very own. I tried my best to be their friend, joined in their little games and played cricket with the boys.

Nothing prepared me for the difficulty the children encountered in discussion. By Wednesday of the second week I was trying to discuss things of interest with them, with little success. Seldom would someone answer with more than a sentence. Some of them gave on-word answers. I noted an appalling lack of ability to concentrate. Some students seemed to be concentrated on playing tricks. I came to the conclusion that learning did not seem to be one of their options in life.

When I asked them to write down their reasons for not discussing in class they had several reasons, the chief of them being shyness and a reluctance to have others laugh at what they say. Some of them were afraid of being wrong. One student expressed fear of the teacher, and about two (one of them tricky Delvan) claimed that they feared that the teacher would flog them—which could hardly be taken seriously.

Two boys, Peter and Ransford—the newest arrivals who lived a good three miles away in Elgin Town, just across from the lovely Lucea harbor—didn't write a word. I asked them to stay in till they had written their opinion. When they showed no sign that I could get anything out of their pens I tried to get their opinions orally. Peter simply claimed that he couldn't discuss anything. For Ransford, it was enough to claim that he had been part of the discussion as late as that morning. I sent them to lunch after fifteen minutes.

After the first two weeks I couldn't claim any great illumination. In fact, I began to be afflicted with more than a little pessimism about the possibility of teaching students with such appallingly inadequate backgrounds. How could one deal with the short attention span aggravated by the little motivation these children had to acquire learning?

Only a year before I had made a study, but only from books, of the problem of providing equality of opportunity in education. In fact, when the government declared "free education for all" in 1973 I had asked for and got an audience with Prime Minister Michael Manley. In about half an hour I outlined how unconventional methods could extend a high school education to all our children—shift systems extended to high schools, less on buildings and more on books, correspondence schools. For the past few years I had been reading Education, a subject I had deliberately neglected in graduate school.

My study in Education had pinpointed the problems that had now hit me smack in the face. These children were suffering from the many intellectual defects that are a direct consequence of a life of poverty. Their home environment was poor, their diet uncertain, and their whole life lacked what could be called a quality of life.

If I had heeded my own study I should have known that you do not begin intellectual stimulation at eleven and twelve.

"Finding the right intellectual climate in the earliest years is an activity to which we should give relentless attention. Psychologists are coming increasingly to believe that the seeds of intellectual curiosity are laid in the early months of life. If the environment is sufficiently rich the child begins to get 'kicks' out of learning soon after birth. Young babies can get hooked on learning very early. The toddler's drive to explore can be encouraged and fed. By paying attention to the early intellectual development of the very young we could prevent the intellectual crippling of thousands of our people. Only a few minutes or an hour at a time spent in the intellectual stimulation of young children can well mean an investment of comparative value in the child's life. A child whose intellectual curiosity is not fed soon stops seeking the pleasure of learning.

"'We get interested in what we get good at,' Jerome Bruner says. Most of our children get very little chance to get good at anything. And the things they are allowed to get interested in hardly go beyond mere survival."

I had confronted the problem of language in my study; but it was still frightening when I met it in the raw. "In the lower-class," I had written, "nothing of importance is transmitted by language. The strongest messages take on non-verbal forms like gestures, intonations and actions while language is reserved for routine messages. Among lower-class mothers there exists between mother and child a paucity of meaning which restricts the child in the central tasks of dealing with his environment. This deprivation must be regarded as a major handicap.

"When we take into account the peculiar Jamaican problem of children learning one language from parents and going to school to find another language that is not treated as such (so close is the Jamaican Patois to English) we see how compounded is the problem. The Jamaican middle-class child will have mastered more or less orthodox English from childhood; the lower-class children never really catch it.

"The general verbal level of poor people is quite low. We are expecting very much of children if we expect them to read and write when they cannot even talk. Differences in middle-class homes and homes of poverty emerge quite vividly when the child is only a year and a half. By five or six slum children and children from backward areas trail so far behind middle-class children that they can, for all practical purposes, be called remedial cases. While lower-class children are getting established in their educational and social rut, middle-class toddlers are forging ahead, exploring the excited world of speech, games and toys under the interested gaze of adults. Curiosity in children of the poor is rewarded by a flogging and the child soon learns that keeping quiet is rule number one for keeping out of trouble. By the time the child gets to school he has suffered a decrease in intelligence."

All this knowledge behind me did not make my disappointments any less. At the close of the second week Edval, Winston and Glenville didn't write the letter summarizing the activities of the week and Lascelles didn't finish his. I asked them to bring two pages on Monday. Most of the other students got started only after some serious pushing. It seems that they had been allowed too much freedom during the day and found the discipline of writing beyond them. I rated my performance a failure.

Joseph's letter did not say very much but contained a confession: "the thing I don't like this week is I was a very bad boy. I rude to you very much this week." Gail was all complaint and confession: "From since the week has began I am not enjoying myself because I am worried because of the grade 7 children. Right through the whole week I have been quarelling with many of the children. I am not a good student some of the times."

Leroy emphasized that he enjoyed Spanish and would like his teacher "to learn me more." Courtney assured me that I "might be the best teacher I ever had". Rose spoke for the class when she said: "I am very glad that you is not beating us in class." Hyacinth gave an indication of the emphasis in the class: "I read many books during the week." But Barbara was looking ahead: "I hope when the end of the term come you will prepare to carried us some where or the other."

Delvan obviously would write his whole letter in Spanish if he could. "Dear Profesor, I enjoyed the week with you teacher. From the first morning I saw you I know that you was a kind gentleman. I enjoyed every period with you but Spanish is the most interesting one. I do not like when you are playing games on us that you are going to beat us that makes us fret. I enjoy poetry and Optional. I love to hear you say that you was going to teach us to drive if you have the time it makes sweet music in my ears." He had written "learn us to drive, crossed it out and substituted "teach" for "learn".

The only real summary came from Sandra, a diligent plodder:

Dear Teacher,

I am going to tell you about The week in Revieue. First in the morning we read news paper and you explain it to us. Then we do some english gramer in the after noon we do some Spanish truesday Mr. Williams teach us some Social study on factors affecting climate, and assignment for nex class. On Wednesday we do poem by ourself on the rain, and the we get a compositionon myself for our home work. Thursday we do mathematics by miss Donaldson she teach us about faction. On Friday we get Reading Reports to make up story by our self and The week in Review by mr. val chambers, and that in (is) the end.

Your same
Sandra Haughton

I was absent from school on Tuesday and Wednesday of the following week. On Tuesday I had to go to the Ministry of Education in Kingston. On a visit to the library at the Ministry I found that they got numerous sample books from publishers who hoped that their books would be used in the nation's schools. I made arrangements to get as many of these books as I could get. These books would go a far way to filling up the little library by my classroom. I did not know at the time that the school had an official librarian, Miss Kerr, so it was without a tinge of self-doubt that I made myself the librarian of Claremont All Age School. The room would be seldom locked, students would move in and out, and books would be read. Of course the children would play tricks in the library, but books would be read, and that would make me happy. The little library became one of the happiest places in the school.

On Thursday I had nothing with Grade Seven but had an interesting experience reading V.S. Naipaul's short story "B Wordsworth" to the combined Eighth-and-Ninth Grade. They sat in rapt attention to a strange and moving story. I vowed to try it on Grade Seven.

Next day I arranged a long walk with Grade Seven. They all joined in with enthusiasm but none of them would walk beside me. So here I was, the Pied Piper walking ahead of twenty students through the village.

We climbed up Baptist Hill which overlooks the coastline at Point sugarcane plantation, descended to Claremont Bottom and went across to Point Road. My mother had lived at Claremont Bottom as a girl. We walked along the tracks passing the homes where some of the children lived. I was reminded again of the poor physical plant that is home for some of these children. We passed two little boys who were apparently alone at home with two dogs which began to bark at us. The bigger boy responded to our plea to contain the dogs by setting them at us. Luckily for us the dogs were more vigorous than effective. Farther down the road we saw Maas Les, now an old man, peering through a window. Mass Les had married my mother's aunt who was now dead. When I was a little boy mother had sometimes taken us to visit Aunt Alice and her husband at Claremont Bottom. Now Mass Les was too old to remember anything. I doubt that he recalled my mother too well though she had once lived with them when she was a girl. To my question to the effect that he should be quite old now he said no— discouraging my trying to find out his age.

All along the way I could not help enjoying the lush vegetation. The slopes of Baptist Hill overlook the sea which seemed amazingly near. The view is unmistakably beautiful, but I doubt the people here think of it. If these people's lives are poor, they are rich in tropical fruits. We picked and ate some guineps and I was lucky to find a sweetsop that had ripened on the tree. We soon reached a little brook surrounded by a thick growth of cocoa plants. The children enjoyed searching for crayfish in the little pools and beneath the rocks.

When we got to Point Road which leads to the sea I had a mini revolt on my hands. We had not prepared for the sea, but all the children wanted to go to the beach, two miles down the road. Delvan had the perfect solution to the problem: the girls would bathe in their clothes and the boys in their briefs. It surprised me that even the most respectable of the girls would have us go. Even Gail who had shown little willingness to go for the walk was reluctant to return "so early," because she did not yet "enjoy myself".

When we returned I found doing something constructive beyond everyone's capacity. I resisted the temptation to ask them to write some poetry. I skipped even asking them to write the Week in Review.

At the beginning of the third week I still felt I was feeling my way. I realized there was no magic formula, only hard work ahead.

I tried to divide Eighth-and-Ninth Grade into groups of their choice, but some found it hard to settle down. I allowed them to move their desks or even to work outside. Few worked with any sense of purpose.

Earlier I had assessed the potential of the students from a story they had written for me:

Henricka: She knows the basics and has good potential.

Carlene: She knows the basics if one excludes punctuation marks. "And" for her is the great connector.

Charmaine: She has much laziness but not much literacy, but is not impossible.

Marva: Her punctuation is poor and her grammar is not any better. Much work needed.

Barbara: She needs much work on grammar. Knows only the basics.

Aston: Succeeded in writing only six lines.

Paulette K: She knows the basics. Can be worked with.

Dian: She can be worked with. She had a point to her story.

Paulette A: Wrote a simple story but shows all the signs of literacy.

Jean: Poor in punctuation. Her writing includes some atrocities like "to sent" and "Janet mother," but not impossible.

Neronie: Same as Jean.

Milton: Beat Aston by one line; achieved seven lines.

Hubert: Shows no sign of trying. Wrote three lines including the phrase "sex mango" (perhaps for "six mangoes").

Hopeton: Wrote a grand total of four lines.

Kenneth: Does little.

Deloris: Her story can be understood. She can be worked with.

Carol: Not much motivation to work hard but has enough to work with.

Doris: Wrote five lines.

Benetto: Wrote three-quarters of a page, but without one period.

Alves: Wrote four lines in which he didn't show much sign of literacy.

Velma: Beautifully clear hand writing but devoid of punctuation.

Myreth: She has enough of the basics and should not resist development.

The assignment today was to recollect Naipaul's "B Wordsworth", a story from the author's *Miguel Street*. The story is about a strange caller who asked a boy's permission "to watch your bees." The man, who spoke correct English, told the boy that he liked watching bees, ants, scorpions, and centipedes. He said he was a poet, the greatest in the world. His name was B. Wordsworth, B for black, White Wordsworth being his brother. "We share one heart. I can catch a small flower like morning glory and cry." He told the boy that he too was a poet, "And when you are a poet you can cry for everything." The man offered to sell the boy the greatest poem about "mothers" at a bargain price of four cents. When the boy's mother refused to give the boy the money B. Wordsworth said: "It is the poet's tragedy." He hadn't sold a single poem. He invited the boy to his yard to eat mangoes from "the best mango tree in Port of Spain." His house was a one-room hut in the middle of a lot. B. Wordsworth and the boy became friends. He taught him about the stars. When a policeman asked him "What you doing here?" B. Wordsworth answered: "I have been asking myself the same question for fifty years."

When the boy asked B. Wordsworth why he kept so much bush in his yard he told the following story: "Once upon a time a boy and girl met each other and they fell in love. They loved each other so much they got married. They were both poets. He loved words. She loved grass and flowers and trees. They lived happily in a single room, and then one day, the girl poet said to the boy poet, 'We are going to have another poet in the family.' But this poet was never born, because the girl died, and the young poet died with her, inside her. And the girl's husband was very sad, and he said he would never touch anything in the girl's garden. And so the garden remained and grew high and wild."

One day B. Wordsworth told the boy that he was writing the greatest poem in the world. He had been working on it for about five years and would finish in about twenty-two years at the present rate. He wrote a line a month, he said. Last month's line was, "*The past is deep*". He hoped, he said, to distil the experiences of a whole month in that single line of poetry. In twenty-two years he should have written a poem "that will sing to all humanity." After that he heard no more of the greatest poem in the world.

To make a living, B. Wordsworth told the boy he sang calypsos in the calypso season. One day the boy noticed that B. Wordsworth looked old and weak. He said the poem was not going well. The boy sat on his knee while he told him "a funny story". The boy was to promise that he would go away and not come back to see him. The story he had told about the poet was not true. The talk about poetry and the greatest poem in the world was not true either. The boy ran home crying. A year later the boy walked along the street where B. Wordsworth lived and could find no sign of the poet's house. It had been pulled down and replaced by a two-storey building. "It was just as though B. Wordsworth had never existed."

My students did a poor job or reconstructing the story though they were so clearly transfixed by it. Some remembered small details like the use of the word "blasted" by the boy's mother but could not reproduce the broad outline of the story; none reached as far as the really poignant parts. Even on a story like this they could muster very little concentration and very little will to work.

# CHAPTER 3

## Crazy to Teach Primary School

On the afternoon of September 27 Carl made a report that some of the girls had read my notes. They had noticed that I would periodically make jottings in an exercise book and were apparently curious about what I was writing. I had left the book on my desk before the class and the girls yielded to their burning curiosity. The culprits I was told were Barbara, Sheila, Hyacinth and Rose.

"No sir, not me sir," Barbara said unconvincingly.

"Sir..." Hyacinth's defense was useless in the face of Carl's relentless accusation.

Sheila sheepishly did not contest, resting her case on the mercy of the judge.

"I was tempted, sir," Rose said.

"All a them listen, sir," Gail told the court. "When the' names came up they love it, sir; and when is something they don't like they defend demself, sir."

Their guilt seemed clear. The only question left was the degree of punishment. Most of the students agreed that some punishment should be given. Glenville, the self-appointed counsel for the defense pleaded forgiveness. And there the matter rested. After all, weren't they in their intellectual rut because their intellectual curiosity had not been properly stimulated? I could not be convinced that their inquisitiveness merited punishment. If they would only read books as eagerly as they read my notes I would certainly be a happy man.

Very cognizant of the ever-present problem of distinguishing between dialect and Standard English I gave the class the following to translate:

"Clemont a one place! It de gwan fram way back—way back fram de days a slavery. People use to work dung a Point fe de white man dem and come back a evenin fi cook, wash and gwan wid a hol heap a tings, fighting and fussin wid one-another, jus like tiday."

Only Delvan gave a creditable translation. Nobody except him made anything, for instance, of the first line, though I had warned them that "Claremont is one place" just would not do. Delvan made it "Claremont is a bad place." For some "a whole heep of things" was good enough. Generally, they simply proved that heir language is not English.

Later I tried the same passage with Eighth-and-Ninth Grade. They seemed delighted that I was so proficient in dialect; but they didn't fare any better than Grade Seven in the translation. There was not one really good rendition of the passage into Standard English. Some used phrases like "a hole lot of things" and generally did very few corrections. In the oral discussion Charmaine came up with Delvan's translation of "Clemont a one place!" But there was little to indicate that these children will ever master the English language.

A story I gave them to write in Patois (Jamaican for "dialect") was quite revealing. Joseph called his story "A story in pat waw" and seemed much more at home in the medium though he still had some Englishisms like "to" for "fi". Glenville's story was written in heavy Patois, spelling and all.

"...the picnie tief him tief till one dae one oman ketch him in a him banana walk da tief him banana."

He could now use similes ("when dem done wid the boy him soft lak a when you beat mango"), something he would hardly have done in English. Sandra wrote her story in (more or less) Standard English, not being able to conceive of the possibility of writing in her native tongue.

When the children didn't know I was listening, I got ample opportunity to listen to the language they really spoke.

"Me gat more chance than you."

"Look right out de so."

"Carl fava ol man eh?"

"Oonu lef de bwoy no!"

"Which work dat? De work wey Mr. Williams gi we?"

In their writing I had to contend with "would teaches," "would taught" and "would sat". One child gave a profound observation in Comparative Religions: "The Church of God will hold up theirs and said amen." The ghost of Mrs. Malaprop elicited this from Sandra: "...because of certain circumcision she did not love him." One child reported that "Jean said her father bought her potato ships." Another wrote of "meat loves and becan" ("meat loves" for "meat loaves").

Rastafarian lingo was evident in Benetto's account of a visit to the zoo where he saw "sinake". "I felt so happy that I did not even want to forward" (return). Marva was apparently expressing the same sentiment: "I realize that I was enjoying myself."

Bennetto's dissertation on discipline in his class is a somewhat close approximation to everyday speech: "...down in the loer grade the children have more discipline than in grade eight and nine when mr Williams is donn here them cant even open there mouth an talk but when he is not here down here is like Bee hive."

By September 29 I was thinking seriously about the problems of defeating ignorance in the primary school system. I confided my observations to my notebook:

"To teach in one of our primary schools is to realize that the whole environment calls for small expectations. Both teachers and students are supposed to expect very little—and of course they succeed.

"A point made by Ansel, a teacher friend, explains the situation very well: Children below grammar school level are not used to doing very much—little homework, no concentrated display of serious work. That accounts, he says, for a kind of disorientation when primary school children get to the New Secondary Schools. Some teachers try to treat them like high school students. It takes them a little while to get used to things like subject teaching and serious homework.

"Books and materials are seriously lacking here. My own feeling is that I should expose the children to as many books as I can. But then getting suitable books on one's own is a very difficult business. Without access to a good library children should at least be expected to have textbooks. A blank exercise book is proving pretty inadequate. It is good to get the children writing, but in order to get anything out of their heads, they will have to put something in."

On the same day I wrote the above musings I gave the Eighth-and-Ninth Grade class a story to write. The story should contain some humor. They should split up into groups. To motivate them I told them I too would write a story. My little story was about Milton and Soneita, two of the least motivated students in the class:

*Milton and Soneita stood by the fence overlooking the blue Caribbean. The trees did not quite obstruct their view, only forming a green foreground for the sea way down below them.*

*"Soneita," Milton said, "who could have known that things would turn out this way?"*

"My dear, imagine anybody thinking, say in 1976, that we would both be teaching at Claremont in 1986?" Soneita was looking up at Milton with soft dew in her eyes.

Milton was thinking more about school now than about love. "Remember, Soneita dear, when I was the clown in Eight-and-Ninth Grade? When I wouldn't concentrate on anything, wouldn't do anything? How times have changed."

Milton was wearing a white pair of pants and a red pullover. Soneita was proud of how smart he looked.

"Hey Milton, remember when we couldn't even speak English?"

Milton was laughing now. "Remember when you used to call me bwoy;wouldn't even speak to me?"

"Pshaw Milton man, do better than that. Past is past."

Soneita was looking irresistible. Her eyes sparkled with intelligence. She had a cool, beautiful, black complexion that set off a radiant smile. Milton held her close to him as the moon peered through the trees at their happiness.

Soneita struggled free and ran to the teachers' cottage to change the baby's diapers. "Boy what a beautiful name you have: Milton Sonito Williams;how you resemble your father!"

The class roared all through the story and cheered heartily at the end. Only a few students were willing to read their stories. Story-telling was obviously a craft they hadn't tried very often. Dian seemed proud of her story about a little boy who was kissed by a lady and declared that he liked love because it felt nice.

When I gave the same assignment to Seventh Grade several students wrote about Three Foot Horse and Rolling Calf, ghost creatures in Jamaican folklore. The choice of theme was probably influenced by the fact that I told them to include some humor in their story. Traditionally a humorous story is a folk story that has been handed down from generation to generation. So in fact what they were doing was to re-tell a traditional story instead of writing an imaginative one.

Practicing to write was already turning out quite good for Lascelles, the oral story-teller of the class. Delvan did not seem to achieve his usual standards, but he had an interesting topic: "How Tiger's story became Anancy's story". The students read their stories to the class, in the main each one preferring to read someone else's story. My own story (about Courtney and Sheila marrying and meeting Delvan the preacher) seemed to have spurred them on. Two stories were quite bold, the "Humor" based on sex. Rose's story included the word "vagina" in the punch line. She said that the story was told by her young aunt (perhaps twenty or so at the time). But the word did not fit into a folk story so I asked her if that was the word her aunt used. "No sir," she admitted, "I translated it."

The morning of September 30 was devoted to Physical Education with eighth-and-Ninth Grade. The period consisted of playing some games which involved vigorous exercise. After the games I asked the students to sit around for a little chat, instead of just going back to the hot classroom for Literature. I talked to them about slavery—the journey from Africa, the revolts (which one or two of them knew about or imagined), and the cruelty of the institution. I showed how deliberate attempts to break up the family resulted in our weak family structure; how white adultery resulted in the brown middle and ruling class still dominant today. They were not too interested in the political aspect of it, but the sexual aspect tickled them a bit. But even that did not lead us very far, for only Doris was capable of any protracted conversation on that, or any other subject for that matter. Every now and again Doris suffered their rebuke for "chatting too much," asking questions, the answers to which she already knew, or some such thing. When I encouraged Doris they would stay around and laugh at the bold questions she asked.

Doris increasingly became my source of information. She was a preacher and consummate actress. If a cast was being sought for a play Doris would be first choice. And she was as bold in her preaching as she was in her acting. Some mornings Doris was asked to prepare devotion. The Church of God Church has had a strong presence in Claremont for a long time and their hand-clapping and lively singing has influenced the style of worship in the school. When Doris took the worship service it was a special pleasure for the whole school. After some lively singing Doris took over and preached. She moved like a preacher, shouted like a preacher and denounced sin like a prophet.

Doris soon became my friend. Whenever she got a chance she would fill me in on the latest happenings the night before, or on what people thought about me.

"Teacher," she would tell me, "you would like to see some of these girls in the night, teacher.... You see how that one play innocent teacher, you should see her last night." And then she would tell me of the sexual escapades of the good, the bad and the ugly. I knew I had to take some of it with a discreet grain of salt.

It was from Doris that I learned that the villagers thought I was some kind of freak. As they saw it I was "psycho," the term they used for mental imbalance. They understood, Doris told me, that I had been to many parts of the world, was very educated, had degrees. They thought I was too qualified for the school. Why, they reasoned, would I want to teach in Claremont school? The only answer was that I was "psycho". Doris or the other children did not share the view of the older folks. Doris said some people thought I was making a great sacrifice to teach at the school. Their view was that I wanted to uplift the students.

Only one person in the village had thought it important enough to encourage me about teaching at Claremont. One day at Meagre Bay in Claremont, Maas Dicky stopped me to say I should keep up the good work. "Bring them up to where you are," he said. Maas Dicky's son, Ken, who went to Rusea's High School has a doctorate and has taught at the University of the West Indies.

Early in the term when Eighth-and-Ninth Grade was forming the class club, Dian refused to be nominated for any position. I thought it was a bad attitude, so I wrote a personal letter to her. Her response:

> Dear Sir,
> I have read your leter carefully and have study all that you have said. I am feeling very happy since you have send this letter to me.

The reason why I did not take any post in the Club is because when the children nominate you them is the same one to curse you. And that is the reason nothing more to say.

Your student
Dian Myrie

Meanwhile I planned with Seventh Grade and Eighth-and-Ninth to produce a newspaper. Gail and Dian became editors. An outline of the items to be included gives an idea of the things on the children's minds:

"Stealing of Goats" (Barbara); Boys holding children—the bad boys of Jericho; Sports (Delvan); Natural Heritage Week (Paul); Lawlessness in Claremont (Gail); Water and Roads (Carl, Clayva, Janet, Gail); What I would like Claremont school to be (Paulette, Neronie, Myreth); Poem (Delvan, Joseph, anyone else); Poinsettia Concert (Dian).

Only Gail's article on Lawlessness has survived:

Claremont is not a peaceful place because people fight and curse one-another. At all times they would come at your home and talk things about people with you. When they leave your home they go back and tell the person what you said and don't talk what they said. When you talk what they said they come and curse you and throw water on you. The people of Claremont need to be put under heavy manners.

# CHAPTER 4

## Flogging and Prunes

During the second week of October I decided to do a lesson with Eighth-and-Ninth Grade on tenses. Perhaps because the boys were out—ostensibly to get grass for Mr. Williams' rabbits—the lessons went over surprisingly well. For this class at least the idea of tense did not seem as mysterious as their writing indicated.

As the month wore on I became more and more convinced that without an intensive reading program it would be impossible to get these students to express themselves with any effectiveness. Noting though that Seventh to Ninth Grade were all weak in punctuation and capitalization I attempted to teach their deficiencies away. Putting in simple punctuation marks, I noticed, presented a huge challenge; but teaching tended to dent the problem somewhat.

I also ventured into the world of agreement between subject and verb. Some of the students—very few of them—were acquainted with the rules, though there were signs that all of them had been exposed at one time or other. In fact, as I was making up my notes after one class, it caught my attention that the Fifth Grade  teacher next door was busy teaching: "A singular  subject takes a singular verb. Do you understand?" I heard her ask the students. I wondered if they would need the same lesson again when they got to Grade Seven in two years.

In late October I gave a test. It was amazing what wonders a test does when students lack motivation. In the face of the test everyone settled down to do something, some of course very little.

## English Test

1. What did you do over the weekend? Answer in about 50 words, using the past tense.

2. Underline the nouns in the following:

It is not honesty to treat people like things.

3. Put in capitals and quotation marks where

necessary:

yesterday i decided to go on tuesday.

you are mad he said to choose an October day.

4. Correct:

(a) You was not here when we go yesterday.
(b) I wants to saw you when you comes back.
(c) Milton with Janice swim in the morning.

I was disappointed that question two, for instance, did not even earn most of the students full marks. A surprising number of the students failed to see three nouns in the sentence, most of them seeing only two. The marks ranged from 14%—71% . The following day I continued with my belief that "Children learn to write by writing" by giving the students an essay for homework entitled, "Sounds I like to hear".

By the first week in November I was complaining: "For a teacher to depend completely on his own resources is an impossibility, and to expect day after day to fire the imagination of country children is a tall order.

"I still haven't succeeded in getting these children to talk, in Patois, let alone 'good' English which they seem reluctant even to try. Neither have I been able to sell them the joy of writing. Writing, it seems, is still somewhat painful to them.

"New things do not seem to fire the imagination. They lose interest very early—regardless of the subject.

"But of course they have their own interests. They fill their time with endless chatter among themselves. There must be a way to interest them in more than the basics of life. So far I haven't found answer."

My policy of not flogging was beginning to affect discipline in my class. The children were used to flogging. All the other teachers in the school did it, and the students simply could not handle the freedom they got in my class. It disturbed me that the children, under no threat from the strap, sometimes found it impossible to concentrate long enough for learning to go on. If I had the power I would outlaw corporal punishment but I was not here to dictate what the principal should do with his school. As the Jamaican saying has it, I was there to drink milk, not to count cows.

Some mornings after worship the principal would line up the late comers to start their day with a few strokes from the strap. In matters like these there is little discrimination; the children from Elgin Town received the same stinging strokes as those from Pond Shop down the road. Some might have noticed that Hyacinth was not regarded as late when house work kept her at the teacher's cottage just behind the school. And for the life of me I could not figure out why teachers, who should be much more responsible, can be excused for being late while little children should be punished.

Things came to a head one morning when Sandra and Joy, Miss Donaldson's nieces who were in fourth and fifth grade respectively got a flogging for lateness. She was furious. After all, she too was late, she said; she too should get a flogging. To the flogging Joseph responded with resentment. Delvan was angry. And Rose was a bundle of fears.

As a child I think my own reaction to flogging ran the gamut of emotions expressed by all the children: fear, anger and resentment. I can remember my own first encounter with the cruel strap. I had just entered elementary school which at the time was in the same yard as the Presbyterian Church (now United Church) at Jericho. I had just returned from gardening on my first Thursday of school. Too small for my six years, I was nevertheless as swift as any other child. I was about the first to return to my bench in the school, was enjoying the freedom of being in class without a teacher and shouting in delirious happiness. Suddenly my whole world came crashing to the ground when "Teacher," the principal, came through the door to find a tiny, undernourished boy bringing joy into the sad confines of his school. After nearly forty years I can still feel those heavy strokes from that brutal leather strap.

The problem of flogging did not go away in our pre-teen years. In the senior grades when beatings became too frequent for our liking we began to discuss whether there was not a law against corporal punishment. We never did confirm whether there was such a law. Now I think the law was only in our imagination. At one time three of us boys decided to respond to the beatings by refusing to cry. We felt big and strong and wonderful when Teacher's greatest efforts were rewarded with a shrug or a smile. Women don't know how deceptive it is when men don't cry.

Fear of flogging almost landed me into a reformatory school before I was ten years old. The beatings at Jericho school were becoming too frequent and my best friend, Camzi, and I, decided the situation was serious enough to get rid of teacher. He was walking home a beautiful girl one Saturday night when we trailed him down the Lucea road from the village square. We would await him in the banana field fifty yards from the post office. A known bad boy joined us, content that if it was something bad we were going to do he would be part of it. Our timing was so badly off that Teacher was thirty yards up the road before we let go our stones. Teacher seemed to have diligently inquired about the two little boys who had followed him. Some boys who had seen us told him they didn't know who we were. Others who were enjoying the usual Saturday night get-together in the busy village square genuinely did not know who the culprits could be. If they had, we would not have been able to sit for weeks. But it was the first and last time I ever contemplated murder. Soon after the episode, I became a Christian.

Despite my abhorrence of flogging though, I surprised myself and the children one Friday in November by administering my first flogging. The children were determined to avoid any semblance of concentration. By the hook or the crook I was going to teach, and some learning was going to go on. The whole class was enveloped in awe as the children saw before their eyes the lamb transformed into a lion. You will have to give it to flogging: it concentrates the mind wonderfully—when fear doesn't drive out all concentration from the mind. One day, perhaps a week later, I was threatening to flog a child when I caught sight of her eyes. They were the most fearful eyes I have ever seen. Suddenly I felt like a tyrant. How could I have descended so low? I, who all my life have abhorred violence had now become an object of fear. I never honored the threat to flog the child, and I never flogged a child again.

I preferred to try another kind of motivation—like this story about Courtney, Sheila and Delvan—Delvan who had told me he wanted to be a clergyman:

*Courtney and Sheila walked into the church where the young preacher was warming to his subject. They had just met on the J.O.S. bus as they had planned. Courtney had made 46 runs in the match against Kingston Club that day. For Sheila, a trained teacher, it was a regular school day.*

*They had been breaking up every two years or so, and Courtney had said the last time that they had broken up for good, but now they were making up for good.*

*That is why they had gone to the church on Queen Street. The preacher was talking about "knowing where you are from". Sheila had a strange feeling that she had seen the preacher before. He was of medium height, was dressed in a white pastoral-looking kareba, was rather distinguished looking.*

*"The boys I went to school with," he was saying, "are now everywhere. Some have myriads of children, some have become teachers. Some of the girls are still doing nothing, knowing as little as they did ten years ago. They hardly recognize that this is the great year of our Lord, 1986."*

*After church, Sheila and Courtney went to see the pastor. They wanted to get married in December.*

*"By the way, minister, what is your name, sir?" Sheila was speaking.*

*Before he could speak, she had hugged him and kissed him rather fondly. Courtney gave him a bear hug too.*

*"Yes," the preacher said, "I am Delvan Jackson."*

One day I was discussing dessert and mentioned prunes. The children had never heard of them. Perhaps I should not have been surprised. When I myself was a primary school boy not far away the wife of the Chinese grocer gave me my first taste of the exotic dried fruit. I promised the children I'd bring some from Lucea for them. The following day I brought a few dozen prunes. The children enjoyed them and conspired to get as many as they could.

The Christmas holidays came and went and school started again in January. In January I was still complaining about how little they had developed in language skills.

"It is quite clear that traditional teaching cannot get to these children. It could work for one or two, but the chief fault of the many is a colossal lack of interest in anything beyond the very basics of life. To hold their interest for half an hour (without the threat of force) could be regarded as a great feat. Decent conversation never goes very far—for reasons beyond lack of interest. How does one explain not being able to carry on a conversation with the boys about cricket in which they are deeply interested?

"The problem of language seems to be lurking somewhere in the wings. When these children communicate they do so in dialect—without any pretensions to Standard English. Trying before their peers demands bravery of an exceptional kind. They claim that if they tried others will think that they are 'spoking'. So everyone is afraid to try. Since any conversation with the barest pretensions to intellectual sophistication is hardly carried on in dialect, the children become rather shy when they see the need to sail into unfamiliar waters."

# CHAPTER 5

## The Lessons of History

Some time during the school year I was sent to Montego Bay to a seminar on Evaluation. I suspect I was sent because it was an obligation and I owned a car. The Education Officer from the Ministry of Education had an M.A. and obviously enjoyed the wonderful terms he had learned in graduate school.

Testing, he said, must be related to (1) knowledge (2) comprehension, (3) application, (4) analysis, (5) synthesis, as in subjective phases of testing (essays, etc.), and (6) evaluation.

I for one did not need this kind of systematization, and most of the other teachers didn't seem to understand it. What I was struggling with in Claremont was how to get some knowledge into my students' heads, not how to evaluate how much they had. According to the ministry official, it is important that there should be control. Why, I wanted to know? For purposes of evaluation there has to be control, he said. What I felt I needed were books and as much enrichment as I could get for my students. But the Ministry, through a pleasant librarian, did provide me with more books than I could hope for, books that had been sent by publishers as samples.

Among the books I got from the Ministry library in Kingston were some English texts for primary schools. Since there were not enough of one text to serve the whole class I decided to use all the texts I could find, each student using his own text or two students sharing one text. For example, Sandra and Janet used *Wheaton's Revision English;* and Gail used *Test Your English.* In Eighth-and-Ninth Henrika and Paulette got *Good Everyday English* as their text, Barbara and Carol *Test Your Understanding of English*; and Doris and Julet got *Written English.* If we couldn't get what we wanted we could use what we had—and use them we did.

Soon our reading program was in full swing. The little library was full of books and the students read many of them. Some joined the branch library in Jericho to find books to supplement their reading. Sometimes during reading period I would sit at my desk and read and invite them to do the same. They began to catch the habit. Delvan was the champion reader. He was afraid of no book, regardless of its size. I could see from some of the expressions in his essays that he was "catching" the language.

By early May I was beginning to test the speed at which the students could write a page. The rainy season had descended on Claremont and it was quite wet. The rain came on the second and on the following day, and I asked them to write as fast as they could on "When the Rain Comes". Delvan wrote his first page in ten and a half minutes. In twenty-five minutes he had finished two pages and his third page came up in the thirty-ninth minute. Courtney did a page in twelve minutes and his second in an incredible thirteen minutes. Joseph came up with a page in 17 minutes; Barbara and Leroy in 21; Carl and Lascelles (!) in 22; Glenville in 23; Sandra in 31; Clayva and Edval in 34; Janet in 35; Gail in 46; Sheila in 49; Peter in 51; and Lintel in 52.

May is not only the time for the rain; it is also mango season. I asked Eighth-and-Ninth to write a paragraph of about 50 words on "Mango Time". The gems I collected were perhaps weak in grammar but rich in sociology and economics:

(1) "Mango time is a very important thing when it ripe."

(2) "When mango start ripe hard we don't want it to eat because we eat plenty a ready. But when mango stop ripe we feel sad."

(3) "When we think of mango time, we then think of belly full, because when mango time we cannot feel hungry any more."

(4) "When the mango is riping we eat plenty of mango we has no lunch. Some time we sit under the mango trees and eat. Some time our tommy get so fill that we caunt even take one more for the rest of the day. So we has to go home."

A concern for the problem of discipline in the classroom was shared by students like Gail. Hyacinth's letter was placed in an envelope and addressed to me at Lucea P.O. Her motives, though, seemed to go beyond the preoccupation with discipline.

Dear Mr. Chambers,

I am writing this letter telling you how the children are behaving in the class when you are not their. The first thing they find to do is play Domino. All who were playing Domino are Ransford and Delvan. So Miss Donaldson tell them to put it down, they put it down but they take the gig and playing it in class. And Delvan Jackson curse bad word in the class. They said that Gail curse bad word in the class but I didn't hear her, but I am not going to say it is true.

The boys who were misbehaving in the class are. Delvan Jackson, Leroy Spence, Courtney Brown, Carl Atkinstall and Glenville Williams, Joseph is the main one. They said they are not paying any money for their mouth.

Your Best Student,
Sharon Campbell

The children did not seem to admire the Rastafarian lifestyle but were fascinated by Rastafarians. For their research project two Eighth-and-Ninth Grade boys chose to interview a Rastaman on ganja (marijuana). They found:

(1) The Rastas believe "the weed don't mad no man". The weed frightens you and people say you are mad.

(2) The weed sells for fifty dollars per pound and retails for fifty cents per stick.

(3) Millions of people including doctors use it.

(4) The farmer cultivates it and the higgler buys it from him.

(5) The Rastas smoke it, getting wisdom, love, knowledge and understanding.

(6) The ashes produced when marijuana is smoked kill germs.

(7) When the Rastaman is cooking he puts some ganja in the pot, convinced that food gives strength and ganja gives health.

Jean, Julet, Charm, Carlene, Paulette, Dian and Doris

submitted research notes which they entitled "History of Claremont".

Mr. Richard Binns told them how united people were in the old days. Some people of the village were fishermen and other farmers. Some people cut logwood which was sent abroad to make dye. People used a cart for transport, rode donkeys and mules, or walked. They lived in houses with ground floors and thatch roofs.

Mr. Thomas Lawrence told them that many people worked on one of three plantations: Hopewell, Point or Georgia. They trashed, tied or cut sugarcane. The memory seemed to go back to slavery when people were tied in ants' nests and were put on *bilbou* (which was not explained). Weaker people were killed and the stronger ones were used to work. The children learned from their source that Claremont was once an estate called Hope Mount. After slavery it was renamed Claremont.

Some had a penchant for dates, noting that in 1851 the Methodist church came into Claremont and the New Testament Church of God in 1935. The Baptist church was built back in 1884. Some remembered the 1912 hurricane and the 1907 earthquake.

Mr. Leolyn Hylton told my researchers that once (no specific date) people worked for four pence per day. He could remember when people cut fourteen heaps of cane for a shilling; then it was twelve and then ten. Another oldster, B. Morris, told the children that once people in the area boiled sugar (made home-made sugar) and little children worked.

We got lurid tales of men being used to draw carts, of beatings, of pregnant women put in ants' nests and people put in the sun for a whole day. In 1809 a pregnant woman was hanged at Point. That explains the pear (avocado) tree now called Belly Woman Pear Tree on Point Road.

Ms. Sylest Wilson remembered when people weeded bananas and sugarcane, broke stone by the wayside, picked coconuts and "chipped" logwood for a living. People travelled on foot, by buggy or cart and by canoes. She remembered when only the Methodist Church was in Claremont. Some men form the village "used to go to Conclegeance to fight war." Boys in the old days wore a long shirt and no pants. People ate Fatten Barrow and Spanish Needle. Most people went barefooted or wore "motor tyre shoes" (a kind of sandal made from motor vehicle tyres). It was usual to eat from the shell of the calabash and to use coconut oil on one's hair.

Mr. Alvin Palmer's date for the establishment of the Baptist Church in Claremont, 1901, conflicted with Mr. B. Hemmings' 1884 date. Mr. Palmer was not the only person to remember the tragic sinking off Point of the the Scottage Dove on its way from Lucea to Montego Bay. Of the 28 people in the boat 16 died, 15 of them from Claremont. The owner of the boat was a Mr. Blenheim. I had heard the story before and can't remember whether Mr. Blenheim was my mother's grandfather or granduncle. Mr. Palmer remembered two hurricanes in 1933, one in 1944 and one in 1951. He said three buildings were erected where the Claremont school now stands. It was not before 1912 that board houses were built in Claremont.

Barbara, Carol and Marva did some research on the history of the school. At first the Claremont All Age School building was a church. Later they built the Methodist Church at another place. There were records going back to 1916. Since then a total of 2,666 students were registered in the school, 11 in 1916, 68 in 1927, 60 in 1939, 11 in 1946 and 67 in the following year. 53 children enrolled in 1954. Each year an average of 44 enrolled. In 1976, 287 students were on roll. The school had seen some good times in the past. Ten years before, in 1966, four students passed the Common Entrance examination and attended Rusea's High School.

Not all the people were responsive to the children's questions. One lady said she didn't want her name to go "over yonder". She didn't want slavery to come back. She was afraid of Castro. Instead of walking up and down, the children were advised to pray. After all they were the ones who would be put in ants' nests.

For comic relief the children did not fail to mention the man who claimed that Claremont was discovered by his great, great grandfather, Christopher Columbus himself.

# CHAPTER 6

## Laughing and Crying

Hardly anything disturbed the rapport of the staff during the school year of 1976/1977. Miss Brown, our pre-trained teacher, who hardly spoke a word to anybody suddenly disappeared. Miss Green came and soon became Mrs. James, a wife of a friend of the school. Mr. Bucknor was a jovial, young, trying friend of the boys. The trained teachers were dedicated professionals—Miss Kerr in grade one and Miss Donaldson in grade five. Mr. Williams had already done his best years but was defeated by ingratitude and what he regarded as the lack of ambition on the part of the people. He had closed his very adequate lab, and his consuming passion was now his birds and his animals, some of them rare specimens. Miss Donaldson who often rode with me as far as Jericho on my way to Lucea was my chief confidant. This was not missed by the children. One day, two grade nine girls, in a very friendly way, came to ask if we were "friends".

The children were very happy when we planned a trip to the beach at Point. They enjoyed themselves tremendously. The boys ignored most of the girls, but for several of the more precocious boys, Barbara was the star. She had a clean skin and a beautiful complexion and a wonderful figure for her age. They were such a nuisance to her that she often appealed to me for protection. In class she was not as distinguished as some of the others, but for one great moment at the beach she was the princess of all Claremont.

The boys were not only very interested in cricket but surprisingly good at it. I judged that they were a notch above the Claremont boys we played against when I was a school boy at Jericho. And they were no doubt better than we were too. With the improvement in communication has come a deepening of the knowledge of the game. Most of the boys knew the rudiments of the game, all the strokes and the art of defense.

I fancied myself a good cricketer and found their pace at their age too gentle to dislodge me easily when I played with them. I hooked and drove and played all the strokes in the book, and they were very impressed. But I found that my own pace bowling had no terrors for them either. I concluded I was no longer the fast bowler I once was.

When I announced that I would be taking them to watch an international match at Jarrett Park, Montego Bay, they were boundless with delight. My car could take four or five but the others would have to travel by bus. When I met them at the Jarrett Park gate some of them at the last moment claimed they had no money to enter. Embarrassed I paid up and cursed human nature.

At the match they sat in silence as if afraid the city would discover them. But you could see that they were devouring everything. After the match they hardly wanted to discuss what they had seen. Once or twice though I caught them expatiating on their stars. For months afterwards those who had had the privilege to go to Jarrett Park became the privileged sports savants of the village.

Late in the school year, I was selected to test Reading in the whole school which had an enrollment of 287. Most students, even a half of those in the remedial class (known euphemistically as "A Special") merited a pass mark of 50 percent. Grade Seven was the star class in reading, thirteen of my twenty students scoring 68 or over. Gail topped the class with 85 percent. Delvan and Leroy scored 75 percent.

My English Language test at the end of June was a fair indication of what I had taught the children.

English Composition
Do one question.
1. Write a story with the last line "I laughed and cried at the same time".
2. Why I like to live in Jamaica or why I would like to live abroad.

English Grammar

I.  Choose the right verbs:
    (1) Everybody (has/have) a book.
    (2) June as well as Jude (go/goes) to school.
    (3) I know that you (was/were) here.
    (4) He (like/likes) to eat mangoes, but they (like/ likes) to eat coconuts.

II. 1. "Will" (as in "will have") is called
       (a) an infinitive
       (b) an auxiliary verb
       (c) a past participle
    2. In the sentence "I want to go to school," "to go" is
       (a) a present participle
       (b) an infinitive
       (c) an article
    3. This is an apple. "An" is
       (a) an indefinite article
       (b) a definite article
       (c) a noun
    4. In the sentence "I have given you time enough," "given" is
       (a) a past participle
       (b) an auxiliary verb
       (c) a definite article

III. True or False (T or F)

(1) The verb form "am" can be used with one pronoun only.
(2) The pronoun "you" always requires a singular verb.
(3) The verb "is" is from the verb "to be"

IV. Explain 4 of the following:
a paragraph, a sentence, an abstract noun, a collective noun, a metaphor, a simile, a full stop, an apostrophe, quotation marks.

Most of the students scored passing marks on the essay, only two students Peter and Marveth, both of whom suffered from infrequent class attendance, failing to reach my pass mark of 50 percent. Rose got a whopping 94% on the grammar test but proved that it was not as easy to apply grammar in her composition. Several of the students like Rose, found some difficulty in my use of the term "abroad".

### Rose's Essay

I would like to live abroad because the situation is much better than in our own country. When you goes to abroad and apply as a citizen you can have your own freedom as the others do. Some of the ways which I think because you gets more pay, clothes and shoes are not so expensive. The peoples of the other country treats you better than your own nation.

When I feel like can go on holiday I would come and visit my friends and families in my own country. Sometimes I would send parcels and money for my families. Many times I would write my friends and tell them how I my life nice and comfortable. I would like to carry all people over abroad.

If Rose and Clayva longed for the pleasures of exile, most of the other students were patriotic to the core. They loved the foods, especially the abundant fruits of the country. Joseph's argument for wanting to live in Jamaica was irresistible, if not altogether grammatical. He wrote in part:

It is not only the fruits…that makes me like to live in Jamaica but if I were born here why should I dislike the land of my birth if one dislike where he was born there is no good in that person. I like to live in Jamaica because my father was born here mother was born here but my gran mother and gran father wasn't born here but anyhow they manage to live here from they were small children. I like to live in Jamaica because it is a very beautiful Country even other people from other Country like to live here in Jamaica if other people like Jamaica why should not I.

Courtney felt he wouldn't leave Jamaica because he was born there, did not have the enormous burden of making new friends and would miss what he called "my coolness" as opposed to the cold weather abroad. It did not occur to him that "abroad" could apply to a tropical country. Edval admired the "plenty food" of his native land. He deplored those who go to England "for one week and they come back they cant speak the Jamaican word Some of them cant speak good." Janet's logic for liking to live in Jamaica was overwhelming: "The reason why I like living in Jamaica is because is there I born and grow and living there." "I don't want to leave Jamaica," she said later in the essay, "I prefer to die here, Jamaica is my nice country."

Glenville had a touch of black consciousness: "I would not like to leave Jamaica because I would not see my black people to talk with and play with and the peoples abroad would not understand my language and I would not understand their." Gail loved Jamaica despite "all the shooting and killing". Sandra's Jamaica was an altogether different place, in spite of the fact that she lived next door to Gail. The tourist board would be proud of her. "We the people in Jamaica have lot of freedom, at night you would have people in the streets till late in the night." She liked the reasonable prices and the fact that Jamaica is "a peaceful place" where you can "walk and don't get hurt from anyone." Of course she spoke the truth about the Jamaica she knew.

Leroy's essay indicated that he could one day grow up to be a political activist like his father.

"We people in Jamaica are very fond of our country. Although many people leave Jamaica and go over broad like England, United States, Canada and other places I am sure that they miss Jamaica. Now I am telling you the reason why I cant leave my country. We cultivate many food crops like banana, sugarcane, citrus, carrot, and more food crops. Although Jamaica is a small country, but not the smallest in the world we Jamaicans are not leaving it to go to other country, it is our country and we must help build it up to make it a better Jamaica. In Jamaica we have many shady trees where we can sit when the sun is hot, and read our newspaper. Jamaica is my country nobody is going to make me leave it. Jamaica land we love."

Delvan's essay was a ringing affirmation of love and admiration for his country, complete with sociological analysis and literary allusion.

"Jamaica is the land of wood and water Not because I am a born Jamaican that's not all that make me love Jamaica. Jamaica have all the delicious fruits that I like. From mangoes right down Coconuts you name them they are my favorite. Jamaica has beautiful flowers right down to beautiful people. Jamaican's national dish is Ackee and Saltfish and I really love that. The people don't live as they should and cause a problem in Jamaica. But I still love Jamaica. Although you might hear about crime committed daily by youngsters, but unemployment cause all those and most of those things, but I love Jamaica. It is the land of wood and water.

As H.D. Cabery said in a poem that we have neither summer nor winter neither Autumn nor spring. Jamaicas flower trees have no special time to beautify the island. Only trees like the Poinciana and a tree that bear yellow flower it and the Poinciana make a beautiful sight red green and yellow or gold. That why I love Jamaica.

The children hadn't mastered the craft of storytelling because they hadn't enough experience to draw from. They needed time to practice. And an examination room is not the best place to create a literary masterpiece. Considering how infrequently they heard Standard English in ordinary life, one should regard their efforts as at least promising. I am not sure if Barbara meant to say the first part of her story was a crying experience and the concluding part a laughing one.

"One Monday morning bright and early I was going to Montego Bay with my friends. When we reached point Road, we saw a lot of Bad Boys standing in a little corner over the hut. We started to fret, Because they used to cut of people neck and robbed away their money. One of the boys turned to my friend and said give me all you have in this Big Bag. The girl said I have no money in my Bag. The boy turned away and said I know if it is true or lie. The bus that we was waiting on came so we take the bus and went to Montego Bay. When we reached where we was going to Over Tan Plaza we saw a old man sitting down at the street side. The old man said please give some of what you have in that Bag The girl gave the old man a Bit of cheese and Bun the man tank the girl for the Bun. I laughed and cried at the same time."

Sheila's work was also unencumbered with the convention of writing in paragraphs. She avoided Barbara's problem with quotation marks by using reported speech. Her mechanics were not perfect but she was becoming somewhat aware of tense, if not all the time.

"It was a sunny day last Tuesday, my mother and I went to the Airport with my Aunt Miss Janet Brown. Who was to plane Air Jamaica to New York. By the time the clock strike 10 we were ready to leave. On the way Aunt Janet told us many things about in the Aeroplane. When we reached the airport it was 10 minutes to eleven, my mother said that we reached very soon because it is 12 o clock my aunt is going to go back to New York. Then my mother buy some ice cream from the ice cream man. when we finish eating the ice cream we started to walk up and down the airport and admiring the thing we saw. Afterwards we cross the road and went over to the other side. And sat under a willow tree fore shade. Then it was time for Aunt Janet to go, she was the last person to enter the plane she stand and wave to us I cried and laughed at the same time."

As the school year drew to a close I began to feel that my time at Claremont was about over. The next year's work would be to teach eighteen students, ten with reading scores in the 40s, one in the 50s, and seven in the 60s—perhaps not dissimilar to the level at which my present grade sevens were a year before. The prospect did not excite me. Would I be realizing my potential if I did not get the chance to organize the whole school on some new pattern? Reorganizing the school on some progressive pattern, taking into consideration the new knowledge now available in the field of education was out of the question. The principal had been kind enough to hire me when no one else would and I was not going to try to run his school for him. When school closed in July, I picked up my books and drove home for the last time.

# CHAPTER 7

## Going Back

In the summer I was asked to head a small high school in St. Ann's Bay run by the Seventh-day Adventists. I balked at the idea at first, wary of the restrictive world of conservative denominational employment. Suddenly, a thought hit me: Why not develop their school into the school I would like to develop on my own? After all, it might not be a princely salary, but they *would* pay me! Why not get paid while doing a service to the community? Though the denomination is normally against sidelines, the president of the Central Jamaica Conference (who automatically became the chairman of the school board) invited me, apparently as an incentive, to bring my printing press from Hanover to St. Ann's Bay (a hundred miles away). What I was not told was that the school was on the verge of closing. I learned later that if I turned down the appointment it would have closed.

The pastor of the church that shares a yard with the school didn't have any faith in the institution and sought a job at the government secondary school for his wife. But the conference overruled him on the ground that it would undermine the school of which he was a prominent board member.

One of the problems I faced was the problem of increasing the enrollment. I tried to improve the quality of staff and sought out promising students wherever I could get them. I gave free places indiscriminately, not refusing anyone on the ground that he or she couldn't pay. I rented quarters for a number of boys who couldn't afford boarding, two of them making chairs and desks in exchange for tuition.

After a year I thought of going back to seek out Delvan.

"How would you like to go to high school Delvan?"

"I would love that," he said without hesitation.

He didn't have to worry about school fees or boarding. Soon the thirteen-year-old was caught up in the new world of high school, starting in third form. In three years he would be ready for his high school final examinations.

During my year at Claremont All Age I had coaxed Delvan into joining the Common Entrance class. He hadn't got a place, and I wondered how this poor little country could afford not to give a high school place to a boy with such outstanding potential. He did brilliantly in his first year, even without getting a chance to write a single essay. I had given his English class to a teacher of some experience who had graduated with a certificate from a government teacher training institution and who had been head of the English Department in a secondary school. This teacher was a brilliant exponent of the chalk-and-talk method. When he lectured he dazzled the pre-teens and teenagers with his knowledge and expertise. The only problem was that the children weren't learning English.

I tried to sell Super English Teacher the dictum that children learn to write by writing. No, he said, the way is to teach grammar first; it is only when you learn grammar that you could then learn to write. Of course, if that were maintained for speaking as well we wouldn't be able to communicate enough to survive. Luckily for Delvan, the talent for writing doesn't die so easily.

With Delvan doing well I went talent hunting again. In the desolate square of Claremont I met Glenville who had left school and had nothing to do. His ambition, he now told me, was to be a mechanic— not just to learn to drive as he had told me when he was in seventh grade. It was now a question of economics. He needed to make a living, not just to have the pleasure of knowing how to drive a car. Would he be interested in going to high school? I wanted to know, dreaming up a scheme to have him join my boys at the den for the poor and ambitious. He turned me down flat. He hadn't the slightest interest in attending high school.

I wondered if he would join the small-time gang of ganja salesmen operating in the village. The children had told me Glenville could easily get contacts in the trade. But ganja trading was obviously not a lucrative business in these parts.

Often during my year of teaching in the area, I had seen a man the children had told me was a dealer sitting in the square, officially unemployed, but probably a small-time hustler. He and I had attended the same elementary (primary) school. He was probably not one of the brightest but was good at cricket. As boys we had lived two hundred yards apart, our homes separated by the home of another family. His family had moved to Claremont and he had lived there ever since. His world, despite the amazing changes of the fifties, sixties and now the seventies, was virtually the same. I wondered if Glenville would be like him. Glenville had enough ability to manage high school but at seventeen (he was probably the oldest student in his class) he could not see beyond the horizon of his little village. Helpless I turned away and left him in his wilderness.

Henricka had won a scholarship to a technical high school, I found out, and Paulette's parents had sent her to Harrison Memorial High School, the Seventh-day Adventist high school in Montego Bay. On one visit I saw Sheila in Rusea's High School uniform, indicating that she had won the Common Entrance.

While I was at Claremont a few students had been awarded a place to José Marti Secondary in Spanish Town—Paul and Dian from Ninth Grade, and Hyacinth from Seventh Grade. There was quite a furor about the school which was built by the Cuban Government, and this area usually voted for the anti-Communist JLP; but the consensus was that politics or no politics no one was going to pass up what seemed a golden opportunity. Not long ago I saw Paul, now a grown young man, planning another direction after having finished José Marti. I hear he went back to England.

Doris, the actress who was my chief informant, had had a baby, I was told, and was living somewhere in Montego Bay. On my second recruitment drive I heard Barbara, the attractive queen for a day, was around, the mother of a little baby. I thought of offering her a high school place in a new environment, but she refused to face me.

Gail's mother did not seem altogether averse to the idea of her daughter going to high school but complained about the money. I assured her it would work somehow. A cousin of theirs lived in the Discovery Bay area, near enough for her to commute. Couldn't we explore possibilities? It was Gail, I think, who confided that her mother thought it was "far", and she did not like the idea of her daughter being away from her. Gail had somehow given the impression that she was accident prone. On a visit to the area, a good while later, I saw her coming from the maternity clinic at Jericho with her baby in her arms.

Meanwhile, at St. Ann's Bay High, Delvan was alternating between being a brilliant student and a violent fighter. One day I warned him of the consequences if he embarrassed me. For a time he curbed his instincts to fight. He became a morose, and demanding "son". When I made arrangements for him to eat at Gully Road, he sometimes refused to go, deeming the quarter mile journey from Edge Hill Road too far for him to travel. He became extremely angry with me for "starving" him. I had paid the fees for him to take two GCE subjects a year early. On the day of one of the examinations I found him in bed, instead of fifteen miles away in Brown's Town in the examination room.

One morning I arrived at the school to find the telephone wires cut. One of the boys who lived at the house with Delvan told me that he had been cutting up things of late. He had destroyed the clothes of a "boarder" of theirs who was really only passing through. This cutting spree seemed symptomatic of something much greater than I could handle. I called Delvan who admitted to cutting up things—but vehemently denied that he had cut the telephone wires. He admitted that he had had enough and welcomed the idea of going home. I wished I had had a home to offer him. Could things really be the end of the experiment? He was ready to go; in fact, he said he should have gone a long time before. I still remember with an emptiness in my stomach the morning I drove the sullen fifteen-year-old a mile down the road to Priory to await a bus. In a few minutes he was gone.

# CHAPTER 8

## Selling but Not Smoking

Not so long ago I got a big surprise. At a youth camp during the Easter holidays of 1986 I met a tall young gentleman who turned out to be Courtney. Now a sophisticated young man he had been sent by an ambitious mother to Harrison Memorial High School, the Seventh-day Adventist high school in Montego Bay. He had developed beyond my wildest dreams and had passed four subjects including English Language at the GCE level—much better than the majority from elite schools who had passed the Common Entrance that he didn't even dream of sitting when he was ten or eleven. He certainly was not up to Common Entrance level when I met him in grade seven ten years earlier, though he had long passed eleven. Later in the year he visited me in Mandeville where I am living and he was studying science at West Indies College. He brought with him an attractive young lady whom he had met in college. He had come because I had told him that I had been working on a manuscript about my year teaching seventh grade ten years earlier. He was fascinated to read about his class, and about himself of course. Courtney finished the two-year diploma at West Indies College and taught at Green Island Secondary before migrating to the States. He eventually became a medical doctor.

Some time ago, Rose, my eleven-year-old star in English Grammar, turned up out of nowhere in Mandeville where I live. Now a petite twenty-four she had gained entrance to Elim Agricultural College in St. Elizabeth after primary school. She had hoped to go on to be a veterinarian but got a dead-end certificate instead. She could not have known that so many of the institutions of learning in her country train their students for low-level jobs and do not expect them to go further. Rose had come to Mandeville because she had become an Adventist and was encouraged to go to West Indies College, the only liberal arts college on the island, which is run by her church. She spent a year and did quite well, the reading habits she had instilled in primary school standing her in good stead. (She told me she once exchanged books with Leroy who also had kept up the reading habit though his education had stopped at primary school.) But the hope of help from her newly-discovered father did not materialize, and she took a low-paying job in Kingston.

Henricka had also discovered West Indies College. She finished the two-year diploma in 1992 and planned to go on to a degree in Business Administration in another two years.

But Delvan's world is altogether different. He had written me for daring to accuse him of cutting the telephone wires. The defiant tone belied his middle-teen years:

Hi: I am warning you to stop thinking that I was the person who had cut your phone. I think I know who your *phone operator* is, but I am not like you people who go about voicing their suspicion without concrete evidence. I am glad you decided against being a law student against your father's wish. You just don't have the qualities of a lawyer—people would go to prison for what they can't even dream about. I am not saying you didn't have reason to believe that I was responsible, because I had cut two other articles with the exception of your phone. Listen, the person who did that badly wanted to see as little of me as possible, or maybe had a Macbeth book for me. I got upset about the over dued return and said things that I shouldn't say, or (the other person) did not like me at all. I am totally sorry that you wasted so much thought on me while I was just not *guilty*. I think your *phone operator* is the very same person who stole a hundred bucks from the school for which I got the blame. Before God I was blameless, before man I had all the blame while the deservor went scotch-free. So long as there is God in Heaven I want you to find the person or persons responsible for all those acts which I stood blamefully for including the Tuck shop breaking. Since you went through all the trouble believing I did when I didn't do the same finding the culprit. This letter is also for Miss Kong. Guess what I am thinking the person who stole your money wanted it for G.C.E. and couldn't pass because it was always bothering (them) or maybe it is in their other *bank book*. I have a list of suspects and as soon as I get to join up with the Police consider them dead if she doesn't confess before that time. I am not taking any blame for what I didn't do while they walked free. You are to be blamed for not taking finger prints when anything went wrong. I excuse that because you don't read any books in the crime club series which I recommend. You are supposed to ask in a form who has two bank book with one having up to a hundred bucks and tell her I had known all along that she was to be blamed for one of the thefts. Please tell her all along she was my chief suspect and that very soon she will be where 'Angels fear to trod.' Take me serious sir. Tell Miss Kong that once she said something to me which I didn't like, and I am sorry for thinking about stabbing her in the back to death. Please tell her how sorry I am. Remember this as long as you live not to trust any body that doesn't happen to be a part of your family, because your mysterious thief was somebody you trusted. I think I have said enough that may help you to find the person for whom I was blamed or have to planned to leave him and her to God. I think you should repay me for the inconvenience you have caused me both personally, physically emotionally, and *stomachally*. I think I should repay you too so everything is at neutral. I wish you good luck not as a friend, because I was hungry too often on your behalf which caused me to Quit. I have gained weight and weight 135. So long.

D. Jackson<br>enemigo

After St. Ann's Bay High, Delvan went to Kennilworth Youth Camp near Sandy Bay, Hanover, from which he was expelled for violent behavior.

A few years ago I met him at Point, on the main road from Lucea to Montego Bay. I was looking out for him for I had heard that he did some business on the coast. He was now a big muscular young man, an unbelievable transition from the eleven-year-old I had met ten years earlier. He seemed mildly happy to see me and matter-of-factly told me that he "sold but did not smoke". Wouldn't he be interested in going back to school? He was at his cynical best in assuring me that he had no desire to be beholden to me again. Didn't he know that his was a precarious business? Wasn't it true that he could get into trouble? And wasn't it true that only "big men" make a comfortable living from the trade? He assured me he would make it. Beyond that future he had no thought.

When I went back to Claremont some time ago I heard that Delvan was mentally unstable. His speech they say is not particularly coherent, but those who play cricket with him say that his standard of play has not diminished. I learned that he eventually went to live with relatives in Trelawny where he was crushed to death by a truck.

The year in Claremont was a great experience for me. But decades later when my students are grown adults I look back on what might have been. With more qualified teachers in the primary school there would be more people to encourage disadvantaged children to try to beat the odds which admittedly are so heavily stacked against them. More of us who only know about misery, poverty and backwardness from books need to try serving in the backwoods for a while. And it will be an unforgettable experience for those of us who once knew what it was like in the wildernesses of the Third World to go back and breathe the air again. That teaching post I took in 1976 was one of the best jobs I ever had. But now I realize that one year is not enough.

www.ingramcontent.com/pod-product-compliance
Lightning Source LLC
Chambersburg PA
CBHW071213280526
45787CB00002B/662